Math on the Job

Math at the Store

Tracey Steffora

Heinemann
LIBRARY

Chicago, Illinois

Edited by Dan Nunn and Abby Colich
Designed by Victoria Allen
Picture research by Tracy Cummins
Production control by Vicki Fitzgerald

Printed and bound in China by Leo Paper Group

15 14 13 12
10 9 8 7 6 5 4 3 2 1

Library of Congress Cataloging-in-Publication Data
Steffora, Tracey.
Math at the store / Tracey Steffora.
p. cm.—(Math on the job)
Includes bibliographical references and index.
ISBN 978-1-4329-7153-3 (hb)—ISBN 978-1-4329-7160-1 (pb)
1. Shopping—Mathematics—Juvenile literature. 2. Stores, Retail—Juvenile literature. 3. Mathematics—Juvenile literature. I. Title.

TX355.5.S74 2013
381.001'51—dc23   2012013374

Acknowledgments
The author and publishers are grateful to the following for permission to reproduce copyright material: Corbis: pp. 6 (© Glowimages), 7 (© Lew Robertson), 10 (© Hola Images), 11 (© Rob Melnychu), 14 (© Lucas Tange/cultura), 17 (© Marc Leon/cultura), 20 (© Helen King), 22 (© Lew Robertson); Getty Images: pp. 8 (Ariel Skelley), 12 (gerenme), 21 (Purestock); iStockphoto: pp. 15 (© Leontura), 16 (© Catherine Yeulet), 18 (© Linda Steward); Shutterstock: pp. 4 (Kenneth Sponsler), 5 (Tyler Olson), 9 (Kzenon), 13 (Wutthichai), 19 (Robert Kneschke).

Front cover photograph of a grocer in a grocery store reproduced with permission from Getty Images (Fuse).

Back cover photograph of a tailor in store measuring length of a man's arm reproduced with permission from iStockphoto (© Leontura).

Every effort has been made to contact copyright holders of any material reproduced in this book. Any omissions will be rectified in subsequent printings if notice is given to the publisher.

Contents

Math at the Store

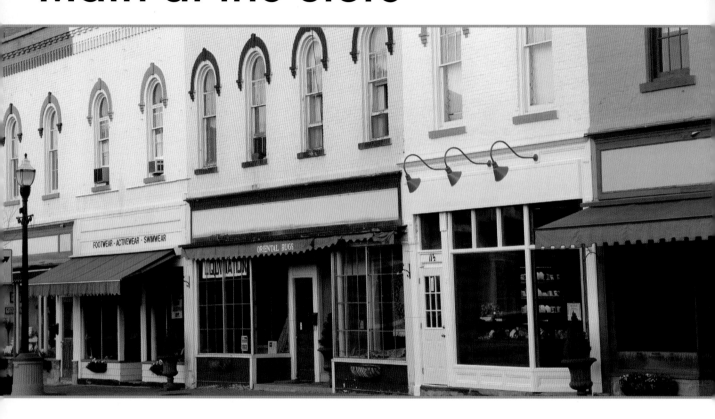

There are many types of stores.

People buy things at the store.

People use math at the store.

Counting

cashier

The cashier counts items.

The cashier counts money.

baker

The baker counts cookies.

How many loaves of bread can you count? (answer on page 22)

Sorting

This man sorts by size.

This man sorts by color.

This woman sorts by shape.

How would you sort these?

(answer on page 22)

Measuring

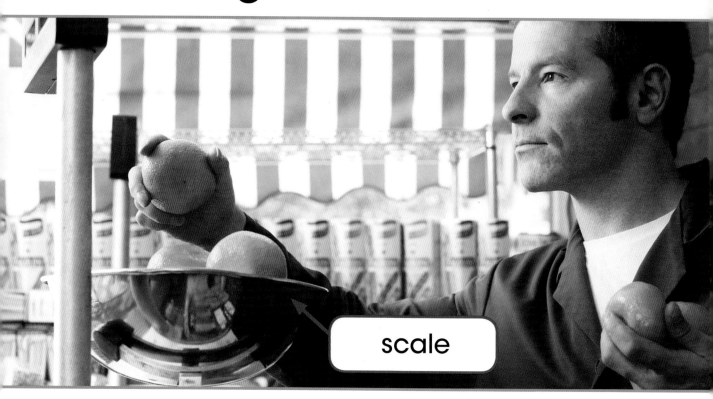

scale

This man measures how heavy.

This man measures how tall.

This woman measures how much.

Are these people measuring
how long or how heavy?

(answer on page 22)

17

Shapes

triangle

There are many shapes in stores.

This woman is holding a square box.

circle

This man works with shapes.

What shape is the bag?

(answer on page 22)

Answers

page 9: There are two loaves
of bread.

page 13: You would sort them
by color.

page 17: They are measuring
how long.

page 21: The shape is a rectangle.

Picture Glossary

cashier person who takes money when you pay for something at the store

Index

Notes for parents and teachers

Math is a way that we make sense of the world around us. For the young child, this includes recognizing similarities and differences, classifying objects, recognizing shapes and patterns, developing number sense, and using simple measurement skills.

Before reading

Connect with what children know.

Ask children to name different types of stores, and make a list (grocery, bakery, clothing store, etc.). Ask them to think of things that need to be counted when shopping at the store or market (fruits, vegetables, cans, money, etc.).

After reading

Build upon children's curiosity and desire to explore.

For parents, involve children in counting, measuring, or sorting items while on shopping trips. Giving them real world experience with math in their environment will help lay the groundwork for further mathematical growth and development.

In the classroom, provide experiences for children to sort and classify items, such as types of fruit, vegetables, nuts and bolts, or coins.